Paperback Quarterly

"Journal of
Mass-Market Paperback History"

Contents

Letters..3

Too Right Bony
   by M.C. Hill...7

Interview with Kelly Freas.......................................12

Recent Releases..37

Repairing Paperbacks
   by Nicholas Willmott...39

Interior Paperback Art
   by Mark Schaffer..43

The Pecan Valley Press
Brownwood, Texas

Paperback Quarterly specializes in the history of mass-market paperbacks. Its goal is to make paperback history more comprehensive and reliable.

Paperback Quarterly features articles and notes dealing with every type (mystery, detective, science fiction, western, adventure, etc) and with every aspect of new, old and rare paperbacks.

Emphasis is placed on the historical research of paperbacks, their authors, illustrators, publishers and distributors, but the editors also invite contributions of bibliographical interest. In short, the only criterion for the editors' consideration is that the subject matter pertain to paperbacks.

Paperback Quarterly pays 1 cent per word (200-2000 words) for articles and notes. Payment on acceptance.

Paperback Quarterly is published in Spring, Summer, Fall and Winter of each year with a subscription rate of $8.00 per year or individual copies for $2.00 each. Institutional and library subscriptions are $8.00 per year. Overseas rate is $12.00. All back issues are currently out of print.

All correspondence, articles, notes, queries, ads and subscriptions should be sent to 1710 Vincent St., Brownwood, Texas 76801. (915) 643-1182.

Published and Edited by

Charlotte Laughlin   Billy C. Lee

Contributing Editors

Bill Crider   Michael Barson
Thomas Bonn   William Lyles

Printer and Technical Advisor
Martin E. Gottschalk

Cover Logo Designer
Peter Manesis

Letters

Dear People,
As editor of MIKE SHAYNE MYSTERY MAGAZINE, I read with interest you article on Mike Shayne in the PAPERBACK QUARTERLY for Spring 1980.

As you undoubtedly know, the Shayne series contin- ues in the short novels we publish every month in MSMM. Our October issue is built around a theme: "Crimes in Other Times" and will feature the lead Shayne story set in 1943. It will have all the wartime background and Mike's wife Phyllis will be a main character in this story which tells how she died. This will fill in an important gap in the Shayne chronology and should be of interest to your readers.

Sincerely,
Charles E. Fritch

(Ed. Note: Though Charles E. Fritch is familar to many of you as the editor of MIKE SHAYNE MYSTERY MAGAZINE, some may be unaware that he is the author of Ace D-367, NEGATIVE OF A NUDE.)

***

Dear Billy C. Lee,
PQ arrived and was consumed in one gulp. The piece on Hitchcock was particularly interesting. Because perhaps I know of a precursor of the Dell

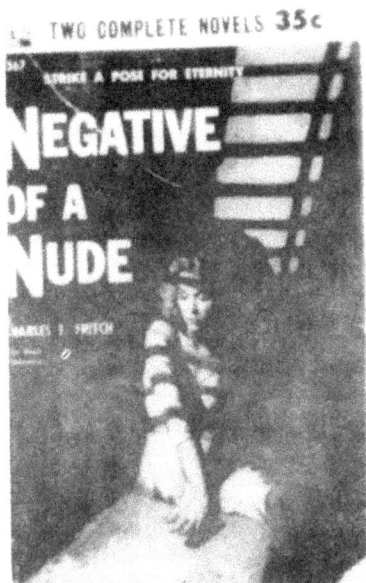

3

items that put the idea into Hitchcock's head --
or some expert packager.
THE POCKET BOOK OF GREAT DETECTIVES (PB #103) is
edited by Lee Wright -- she acknowledges the help
of Boucher and Queen; but the rather meaningless
two page introduction has the signature "Alfred
Hitchcock." Surely his $1000 did not start here.

Regards,
Charles Mac Donald

***

Dear Billy,
The last issue was superb, a great mix. As you
know, I agree completely about the need to collect
reprintings. And tell Charlotte that Larry
McMurty has the reputation in Washington, D.C. of
being a snob.
By the way, Rolla MacDonald edited (maybe) the
first Hitchcock anthology. I don't know who did
the cover.
I wish Bernard Drew had included a list of the
Shayne books that Robert Terrall did. Terrall uses
other pseudonyms, including "Robert Kyle" (for the
Ben Gates paperback mystery series he did for Dell).
The homosexual art director he mentions has to
have been at Dell, since they published the Mike
Shayne books. I'd like to know who else besides
Terrall and Dresser did the Shayne books. Ryerson
Johnson did at least one, but who else?
Altogether, a fantastic issue.

Best,
Bill Lyles

***

Re- Pocket Books #3, LOST HORIZON, James Hilton.
    The 38th printing (March 1952) has the same
cover as the 43rd, the khaki clad soldier and
woman.

4

Your comment about Gertrude on the cover isn't clear to me. It reads as if you are saying Gertrude was on **all** printings through the 34th. Early Pocket Books had the "25¢" mark in the lower right or left (it varies) hand corner of the front cover instead of Gertrude.

I can't tell which Pocket Books number was the first to have the logo on its first printing, but number 23 (AUTOBIOGRAPHY OF BENJAMIN FRANKLIN) has the price on the first printing and number 34 (GULLIVER'S TRAVELS) had Gertrude on the first printings. I don't have numbers 24 through 33. ...At some point in time reprintings of the early titles would have the logo substituted for the price, but Pocket Books was not consistent on when they made the change,..

Yours very truly,
Charles C. Culpepper

(Ed. Note: I am very glad you have written in this regard. It points out clearly the importance of later printings to get the true and total picture of paperback publishing history.

You are quite right, my comments about Gertrude on the cover of LOST HORISON are unclear. When I said, "Through the 34th printing (July 1945) Pocket Books maintained the original Steinberg cover ..." I was simply referring to the Steinberg cover illustration being used on the 1st to the 34th printing. My next sentence however says that Gertrude was featured in the lower right hand corner of the book. Here I was thinking (though not saying unfortunately) of the 34th printing rather than 1-34. There are at least nine different covers of LOST HORIZON. These will delineated in up-coming book by Thomas L. Bonn.

The first printing of LOST HORIZON features "25¢" in the lower right hand corner instead of Gertrude.)

***

Dear Editors:

I recently received Vol III, No 1 of PAPERBACK QUARTERLY and I think it is the best issue yet, except for one thing. I miss the color. What happened to the color? Anyway, the articles, interview and black and white pictures are superb.

I especially enjoyed the Barson interview with Michael Avallone and Bill Crider's piece on Avallone. Also, I liked the article on the Hitchcock: Dell collections. There would have been a good place to use your color.

By the way, I happen to have a slightly battered copy of "Ed Noon and the Bouncing Betty," the seemingly same magazine mentioned in the Avallone pieces and it is one the gems of my collection. But, I hadn't heard of "Ed Noon and the Alarming Clock" until now. Now, I'm on the trail of that one.

Best Wishes,
Robert M. Williams

***

THRUST

SCIENCE FICTION IN REVIEW

THRUST ----- Science Fiction in Review is published three times a year and contains items of interest to collectors of Science Fiction paperbacks in particular, including reviews of recent paperback originals and interviews with well-known science fiction authors. With a fine mix of regular columns, letters, and artwork, THRUST belongs in your library. Subscriptions are $5.00 for four issues and are available from Thrust Publications, 11919 Barrel Cooper Court, Reston, VA 22091.

Too Right Bony
by M.C. Hill

If you are a newcomer to the mystery genre,
chances are good that you have never heard the name
"Arthur W. Upfield."

Mr. Upfield was born in England, September 1,
1888, the eldest of five boys. He was a daydreamer
who failed in most tasks set before him, causing
his father to ship him away to Australia in 1911.
Here he fell into the ways of the outbacker and became a boundary rider and a drover which led him
into wondering all over the continent. When World
War I broke out he joined the Australian forces and
served five years in Gallipolli, France, and Egypt.
During this time he married, and he and his wife
had a son named Arthur James. After the war, he
returned to England and settled down for a short
while, but he could not forget his adopted country
and soon returned to Australia.

He once more became an itinerant worker (swagman), pearl fisherman, cook, gold miner, etc. For
three years he roamed over most of Australia making
many friends. Having a keen analytical mind, he
learned to observe and store away thousands of facts
about the back country, the animals, customs and
habits of the natives; and he also learned to speak
the language of the aborigine.

During his travels he contacted and made
friends with a family who had lost their son in the
war. He spent a great deal of time with them, and
they encouraged him to write and to quit wasting
his time roaming the country. While supporting
himself working as a cook, he wrote THE BARRAKEE
MYSTERY. He was disappointed when it was rejected
by a literary agent, but he went back to work and
wrote the novel THE HOUSE OF CAIN, which was comple-
ted, submitted, accepted and published in 1926.
With this encouragement, he re-wrote THE BARRAKEE
MYSTERY, and this time it was accepted and published in 1928. This book was published in the United

States by Doubleday as THE LURE OF THE BUSH.

Mr. Upfield continued to travel throughout the major provinces of Australia, and he turned out at least one book a year until his death on February 13, 1964, in his seventy-fifth year.

From 1926 till 1964, he had thirty-three novels published, twenty-nine of which featured Inspector Napoleon Bonaparte. Of the thirty-three novels published, eight have appeared in the United States in paperback form. Berkley Medallion published the first four of the following titles in 1963 and the other four in 1964.

F831 DEATH OF A LAKE
F832 THE BUSHMAN WHO
          CAME BACK
F850 MURDER MUST WAIT
F859 VENOM HOUSE
F913 THE NEW SHOE
F916 THE WILL OF THE
          TRIBE
F927 SINISTER STONES
          (CAKE IN THE HAT BOX)
F1020 WINDS OF EVIL

Pacific Books, the Australian publisher, did the following eight titles in paperback.

THE SANDS OF WINDEE
MR. JELLY'S BUSINESS
THE WINDS OF EVIL
THE BONE IS POINTED
BUSHRANGER OF THE SKY
DEATH OF A SWAGMAN
THE DEVIL'S STEPS
AN AUTHOR BITES THE DUST

Pan Books Ltd. of London produced the following sixteen paperback titles.

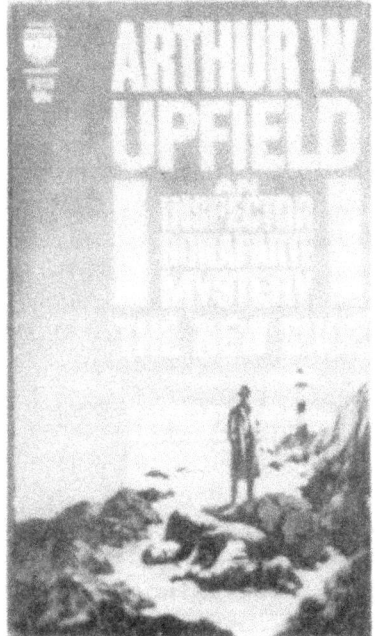

8

THE BARRAKEE MYSTERY
WINGS ABOVE THE DIAMANTINA
MYSTERY OF THE SWORDFISH
     REEF
THE MOUNTAINS HAVE A
     SECRET
THE CLUE OF THE NEW SHOE
MURDER MUST WAIT
DEATH OF A LAKE
CAKE IN THE HAT BOX
BONY BUYS A WOMAN
THE BACHELORS OF BROKEN
     HILL
BONY AND THE BLACK
     VIRGIN
BONY AND THE MOUSE
BONY AND THE KELLY GANG
BONY AND THE WHITE
     SAVAGE
MADMAN'S BEND
THE LAKE FROME MONSTER

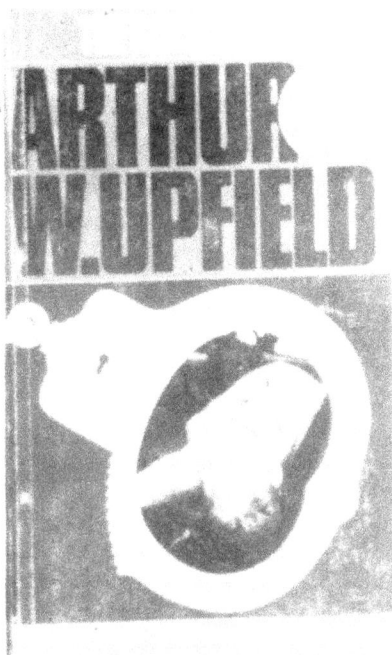

     THE LAKE FROME
MONSTER, Upfield's last
book, was left unfinish-
ed at his death, and it
was revised and finished
by Mrs. D. Strange and
Mr. J.L. Price.
     One of the most
difficult titles to
locate in the United
States is THE DEATH
OF A SWAGMAN published
by Signet as #658 some-
time in 1948. Nearly
all of Upfield's titles
are difficult to locate
in paperback form as
you will learn when

9

Arthur W. Upfield

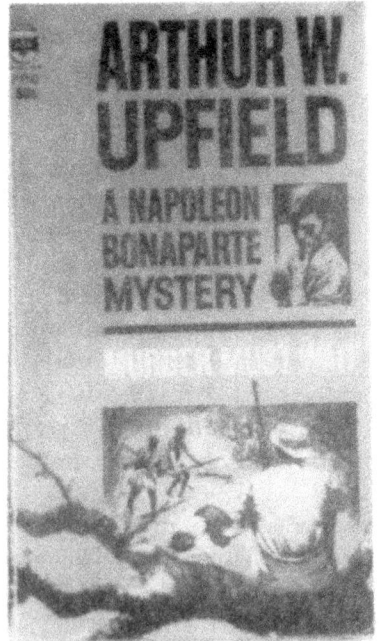

you try to uncover them. Fortunately Doubleday has
reprinted nineteen titles in hardcover here in the
United States; and with a little luck, you can purchase them through your favorite bookman. Unless
you are well-fixed financially, forget about the
British first editions which were produced by
Heinemann, Angus, Aldor, or Hutchinson. They are
seldom offered; and when they are, prices are high.
Your best bet, if you are a reader is to be happy
(as I am) with the paperback editions. These can
be purchased for from $1 to $5 each, depending on
printing, condition, scarcity, and demand.

Read one and I will almost guarantee that you
will start looking for the others. They are con-
tagious, the major reason being that Upfield placed
his hero in at least four of the five major provinces
of the country so every story takes place in a different locality with new and varied character situations,
times of the year, and with Bony assuming various
disguises, aliases, and roles to better cope with
each new case. Upfield successfully manages to
have Bony bring each culprit to justice while avoi-
ding the stigma of being repetitious or becoming
camp--Too right, Bony!

PULP 12

Of special interest of pulp collectors is Robert Weinberg's
Pulp 12. Published as a tribute to the western pulps, *Pulp 12*
contains letters from western pulp writers Harold Cruicks-
hank and Walker Tompkins, an article by Nick Carr entitled
"Contemplating the Pulp Westerns," and superb western art by
Frank Hamilton. This 32 page publication also contains a re-
printing of an Avenger story,"Cargo of Doom" by Kenneth
Robeson. *Pulp* is not available by subscription but single issues
can be purchased for $2 each. For more information write to
Robert Weinberg, 15145 Oxford Drive, Oak Forest, IL 60452.
Please enclosed S.A.S.E.

Interview with Kelly Freas

The following interview with cover artist Frank Kelly Freas was taped in March 1980 at Aggiecon XI of Texas A&M University, where he was artist guest of honor. Kelly Freas holds an all-time record of having been nominated for seventeen Hugos and awarded ten. All readers of science fiction are familiar with the dominant foregrounds and vivid treatment of color that characterize his works. And even people who have never looked at a science fiction book or magazine may have seen his poster depicting the space program which hangs in the Smithsonian Institution.

PQ: Although PQ is primarily devoted to the history of mass-market paperbacks, we're interested in the Starblaze trade paperbacks that you and your wife Polly are associated with. Do you actually own the publishing house, or what is your role in this publishing venture?

KF: *No, we were just employed by them. Of course, we are no longer associated with the line. We were just too busy to continue--busy with a number of other things last year.*

PQ: We were wondering about the distribution of Starblaze Books. We see a mailing address here on the flyer. Are the books only available through mail order?

KF: *It was originally intended to be a strictly mail distribution, but what with the cost of handling and the feeling we had that bookstore distribution, displays, planned-purchase displays and* stuff like that--we felt we had to go that way. And well, frankly, after the CAPRICORN GAMES distribution, we've had some difficulties. They have a wonderful man now, and they'll soon get back onto a regular schedule.

PQ: Today, in your lecture, you mentioned that about 30% of the color and detail in a painting is lost in cover reproduction. As an artist, did you find that more pains were taken to faithfully reproduce your paintings in this special line of trade paperbacks than are taken in reproductions for mass-market paperbacks?

KF: Oh, much more. Where the mass-market paperback will cost maybe 7¢ to produce, in a small line such as Starblaze each book costs $1.65 a piece-- actual production cost.

They use one of the best coverstocks. It's practically indestructible. You can give it to a baby to cut his teeth on and still have a cover. And the back is both sewed on and glued; it'll never shed a page. The backing used is supposed to be good for a million flexings. The paper is acid-free paper. All of these things were taken into consideration to produce the very best possible book for the money. We had decided that $4.95 was the top price a science-fiction reader would want to pay for a paperback book; and evidently, we were right because everybody else is picking up the same idea with their over-sized and illustrated paperback editions. Even so, ours were better because essentially they are a hard-cover book with a soft-cover binding. They could have been bound up just as well as hardbacks.

PQ: We noticed the brown tones and other shades of ink used for the printing as well as the illustrations in Starblaze books.

KF: In cases where I used a brown for the illustrations--I used another one in green--I changed these each time. It's the same thing, but it gives you the feeling of color, while you still get a good readable type. This is loaded with just about 30% green into the black. And it works very nicely in half-tones, too, because it gives you a feeling of color.

PQ: Did you choose the color of ink to fit in with the book title?

KF: Basically, yes.

PQ: We notice that your wife is also listed as associated with the production of Starblaze books. Is she also a cover artist and illustrator?

KF: No, she gets the ideas, and I put them on paper.

PQ: Did you two actually read the manuscripts and work together on publication decisions?

KF: In all cases except in the actual painting of the picture. Although we had no first reader, we read all the manuscripts, and accepted or rejected them on the basis of simply whether or not we enjoyed them; we were interested essentially whether it was actually a good story. We are not "literary" in the usual sense of the word, so we were going entirely for story values, and inescapably, for visual values. One story I did turn down and hated to because it was just loaded with picture ideas, but it was not useable for this type of format. It presented a whole series of short stories, but otherwise it told the reader more about dinosaurs and such things than the reader really wanted to know.

PQ: You said that you are no longer associated with Starblaze Books?

KF: Yes, we have no connection with them after #10.

PQ: Were there differences of opinion that led to your leaving?

KF: I wouldn't say that. My wife's health is our main consideration. Our leaving was mostly a matter of too much pressure for time. When you work fourteen hours a day, you're running steadily!

PQ: In your book, FRANK KELLY FREAS, THE ART OF SCIENCE FICTION, you wrote: "I came into science fiction at precisely the time the old pulps were folding; paperback science fiction was just beginning to raise its head..." What was the first paperback publisher that you did cover art for?

KF: I started to say it was Ballantine, but I may have done one earlier for Avon. I would have to check back, but I think it was probably Ballantine.

PQ: In your lecture, you said that cover artists and illustrators are sometimes limited in their expression by their editors. Which paperback editors do you most like working with?

KF: I don't like any of them, to be truthful! [laughing] Oh, I'm just joking , of course.

PQ: How did you break into doing paperback art? Did you just decide that you wanted to do paperbacks?

KF: No way! I had tried back in about 1952, and it didn't work. And at the time I started doing them I was in a position where they called me. In fact, I got a lovely letter from Don Wollheim asking me to come in and see his art director and explaining that Ace was the biggest science-fiction publisher in the business. I was really pleased with this because it had only been ten years before that he had looked at my stuff and said, "Naah!"

PQ: When you started out with your first paperback cover art sales, did you talk to the editor or the art director, or how did you go about making the sale?

KF: *Ordinarily what will happen (it seems to still be the case) the editor may run across your work because he's the science-fiction reader. He'll run across your work in something else and say, "Hmmm, I'd like to have this guy." So he'll call you up and find out if you'll go along with the gag, depending on whatever it is that the budget is. You usually go in and talk to the editor like that; then he introduces you to the art director. Mostly, in the paperback houses, from that point on, you work with the art directors.*

PQ: In your lecture you said you liked art directors the way you liked your authors--dead. Do you have a favorite art director?

KF: *Me!*

PQ: You've said that John W. Campbell, Jr., was your favorite editor in science fiction magazines. Do you have a favorite editor among the publishers of science fiction paperbacks?

KF: *Probably the easiest one I've had to work with and the most all round pleasure is Donald Wollheim. He and I think very much alike. We like the same covers; we like the same sort of science fiction. We both have a predilection for pretty girls and rowdy-dowdy adventure.*

PQ: You've done cover art and illustration extensively in both the pulps and paperbacks. Do you find that the artist has more freedom in one publication medium than in the other? Are the editors or art directors of one type publication "pushier" with the artist than the editors of the other?

16

KF: I would say that in a large measure there was more freedom in the pulps--although you wouldn't think so to look at the old magazines. You were working to a formula, but it was a fairly flexible formula, ant anything like as rigid as, say, Laser Books were. The formula was more a verbal one: "You've got to have a bug-eyed monster; you've got to have some gadgets; you've got to have a pretty girl; you've got to have a husky her." OK, this is what the reader expects. From then on the way you put it together is limited only by the amount of type lines you can squeeze in.

PQ: How much freedom do you have in paperback art?

KF: In most paperback books--and it's worse out of science fiction than it is in--there is very little freedom in the covers because they're usually de-cided on by committee. The art director does all the work, but somebody else has the final decision. And usually these guys making the final decision know absolutely nothing about art. For instance, in packaging, they may insist that you cover all of your work to fit whatever their packaging agent says.

PQ: So you have to make allowances for what will be written on the cover itself?

KF: Yes. If you don't, you're in trouble. I paint allowing for at least an inch on all sides of the image area of the picture on a book of mass-market size. Not blank space, but space that it doesn't matter if it gets cut off. And even so they will, one way or another, find some way to crowd it out.

PQ: They tell you in advance what size they need or do they simply reduce it?

KF: Oh, yes. They reduce it, but it has to be drawn in proportion.

17

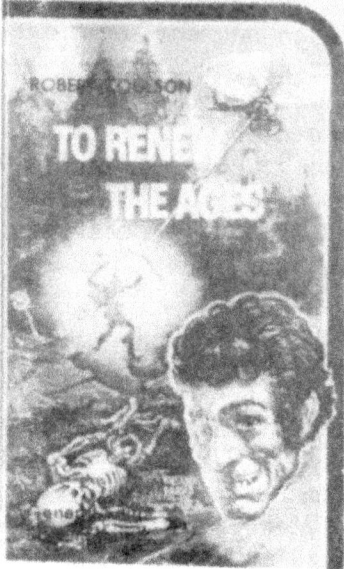

26

ROBERT COULSON

TO RENEW
THE AGES

Laser Books 48

REBELS
OF MERKA

AUGUSTINE FUNNELL

Books 49

TIGER IN THE
STARS

Laser Books 45

FINISH LINE

STEPHEN GOLDIN

PQ: They tell you to leave the top fourth, or whatever, of the painting without any central images?

KF: Yes, Always leave a lot of room at the top. In the case of Laser Books, everything was specified: the distance of the chin from the cut off, the distance of the outside edge of the head from the trim-line; everything was figured right down to the last fraction of an inch. And I even had graphs that I could lay over the picture; they were on acetate so that I wouldn't by mistake run out of space. You can look at the Laser covers and see how they were actually painted, done on matwork--by the way, that was Polly's idea and her production. She laid out the first eighty books, picked out the colors on little pieces of matwork cut in proportion to the design, laid them all out, pasted them up on a board, so that regardless of how they were displayed you were going to get no two of the same color. So that this way we had all eighty of them laid out in advance.

PQ: Since we're talking about Laser Books and most of the readers of PQ are paperback collectors, could you explain the purpose and distribution of the special edition of SEEDS OF CHANGE, by Thomas F. Monteleone?

KF: Yes, the "Limited Collector's Edition is what you're talking about. They printed 10,000 of them ,which in their terms is a very small edition. This was a funny one because they paid the author royalties on 10,000 copies; and then gave them away. And the author was furious because he was quite certain that they were producing a lot more than 10,000 copies.* If the thing had been as

---

*The editors of PQ must side with the author. In a recent book-buying trip through Texas, Arkansas, Tennessee, and Pennsylvania, we found this book to be the most readily available of all Laser titles.

19

successful as they expected, it would have sold more. Actually they got into about 40,000 sales. To anybody else 30,000 copies would have been well worthwhile, but when you're used to selling 90 to 110 thousand copies of a title, this is small potatoes. They said, "Forget all this. Let's put our money into the things that will bring us back some profit." So they went back to the Harlequin Romances, and eschewed science fiction entirely.

PQ: You were the exclusive illustrator for Laser Books for two years; is that right?

KF: That's right.

PQ: You did every book?

KF: I did 67.

PQ: Do you ever do the lettering of the titles themselves?

KF: I used to. I was weaned on commercial art, and hand-lettering is an absolute necessity in that work. Well, for instance, I did a lot of TV work, television advertising; and if I had to buy lettering from somebody else, I couldn't have made a dime out of it. I did farm out a lot of stuff for show art, but the actual precision lettering I did myself. I was not fast enough to make it more profitable to do it myself. Nowadays, most things are paste-ups, transfers, overlays, something like that; there's very little hand-lettering done on any of this stuff.

PQ: Has a paperback publisher ever asked you to put lettering in at a certain point...?

KF: No, but what they do sometimes is to ask me to specify what kind of type, and then what I usually do is draw it in on a layout the way I think it should go and write in also what type face that they can refer to in their type speciman books to get exactly this effect. That's as far as I go to do lettering.

PQ: Do you feel that the lettering is a big part of the art itself?

KF: Ideally, it should be, but in paperbacks it isn't. The only concession is the area that you leave for the lettering to be put in. But that is one of the main differences between a paperback cover and a book jacket. On the book jacket the lettering is a basic visual element that is worked directly into the illustration, and it's a total concept. Some of this is beginning to filter down to the paperback market in, say, maybe the last four years, but mostly the type is machine done. Sometimes you'll find a cover is all type, in which case it is sometimes set out--mostly even that can be done on a machine that will stretch it, squeeze it, do anything you want to, rather than hand-lettering.

PQ: I wonder why a marketing director would want to have all lettering on a cover. It seems that cover illustration really helps sell the books. What is the reasoning behind having only lettering on a cover?

KF: Their reasoning is display value. Remember these books are in competition with a whole rack. If everyone else is using dark, illustrated covers, a white cover with red lettering and maybe just a little black on the edges will stand out like a sore thumb. You've got more display value than if you got Michangelo himself to paint you a cover.

PQ: On WARRIORS OF DAWN, we noticed that the

21

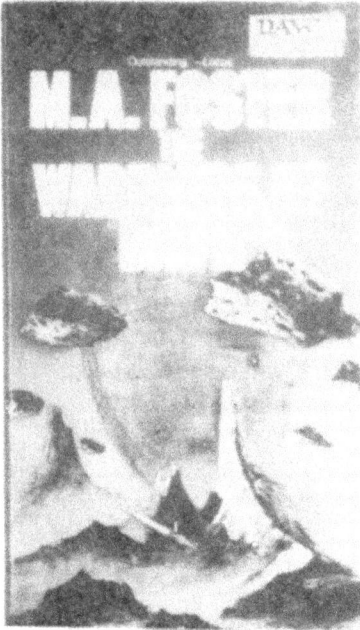

Warriors of Dawn (3rd printing)
[Note Reversed Cover]

Wariors of Dawn (1st printing)

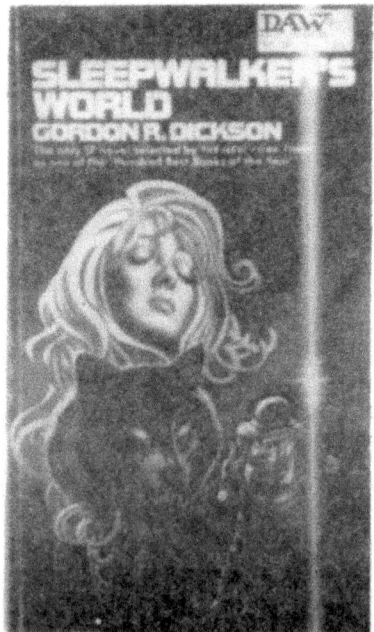

lettering comes nearly half-way down the cover
and intrudes on the painting.

KF: *Oh, that is a concession to the DAW emblem
in the upper left corner. But this edition is
considerably better than the first one. In the
first edition some creative art director took the
title, WARRIORS OF DAWN and put it right around
the top of the spaceship! And I just flipped!*

PQ: So there's a variant cover of WARRIORS OF
DAWN?

KF: *Yes, they changed the type on this second one.*
[He's examining a copy as he talks.] *And wait a
minute! They've reversed it too!*

PQ: We noticed that your signature was backwards.

KF: *I thought there was something strange about
it. It finally registered!*

PQ: We were going to ask if that reversal was
intentional or a mistake.

KF: *As far as I'm concerned it's a mistake. From
that standpoint of a publisher, that's making new
use of negatives, transparencies, that he has. I
think it was done intentionally to give a different
look to the second cover.*

PQ: Then the.re may have been three covers: one
with the title around the spaceship, one reversed,
and one right. Or was the reversal the only way
the picture would fit beneath the lettering? It
may be that turning it over, they could avoid push-
ing more lettering into the boulder.

KF: *That's right, if it were the other way they'd
have problems.*

PQ: Turning to a consideration of your Laser covers, I've read in your book that you painted a picture for Laser Books before the format was set. Then you explain that you added the head inset on an acrylic panel so that the original painting wouldn't be changed. Since you were responsible for establishing the Laser Format, how did you happen to paint the picture before you developed the format?

KF: Well, there were three covers which just coincidentally had the face, and all of a sudden that idea of the big face took over. Remember, you're dealing with the people who publish Harlequin Romances. You know what those look like; they're just straight pretty-girl covers, period. So naturally, if I had realized what I was getting into, I would never have let them see that. But as it turned out, the big face just registered, "Bang! This is our sort of thing." And from then on we were stuck with it. The readers hated it really. The stories incidentally were very, very good until they went into print. Being, as they call themselves, book pushers, they slashed everything, regardless if it were 90,000; 75,000; or 100,000 words. There was one story of 125,000 words which they cut into two books. With the others they just mercilessly slashed out 25 to 30 thousand words. And it sometimes made it very difficult to follow the plot.

PQ: Do you read every book for which you paint a cover?

KF: Oh, yes. I read every book three times. First straight through, just as a reader. Second I go through with a sketch pad in my hand, and make notes, get ideas for black-and white covers. I like to plan out black-and-white first, and do the cover after that. But it doesn't always work that way. And then the third time I go through is

24

to check the actual details. By this time I've got
my sketches worked out so that I know what's actually going to be there. But I want it to be right.
If there's a gun, I want to know how it's described.
I don't want to put in a blonde where the author
specified a brunette. I try to get things as
exact as I can. But no matter how hard you try
you're going to blow it every once in awhile. For
instance, on this one [TO RENEW THE AGES, by
Robert Coulson, Laser #26], I didn't blow it, but
everyone complained about the fact that I reversed
the man's face. I had to. This side of the man's
face had been burned away; it was all scar tissue.
If I had done it the other way, I would have had a
horror picture, not science fiction. So I had to
change it on the cover. Of course everybody wanted to know why I got his face backwards. That was

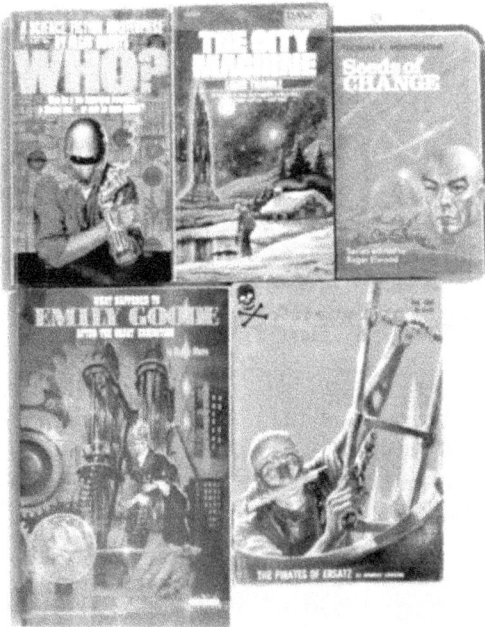

Who? by Algis Budrys (Lancer #73-810); *The City Machine* by
Louis Trimble (DAW #24); *Seeds of Change* by Thomas F. Montel-
eone (Laser Books #1); *What Happened to Emily Goode After the
Great Exhibition* by Raylyn Moore (Starblaze #1); "The Pirates of
Ersatz" by Murray Leinster (*Astounding Science Fiction*, Feb
1959)

it. It had to be that way. But there are lots of times that it's purely oversight. You try to think of everything at once, but you don't quite make it. This costume for Emily Goode [WHAT HAPPENED TO EMILY GOODE AFTER THE GREAT EXHIBITION, by Raylyn Moore, Starblaze Books], for instance, is accurate; but just barely. If I had missed it by another two or three years it would have been hopeless, because the bustle vanished and the whole style changed. I didn't find this out until after the picture was finished!

PQ: In your book, you mention the research on black holes that you did for the illustration of "Hero" in ANALOG. Do you do comparable research for details such as dress fashions?

KF: Oh, yes. For anything that requires historical costumes or instruments, that sort of thing. I try to be as accurate as possible. And it's also helpful in developing future costumes, because by the way the culture is described (even if the author doesn't go into any discussion of the dress) you have a pretty good idea of how the fashions will follow the culture described. Of course, my wife tells me that the only reason I'm a science fiction painter is that it gives me an excuse to do the research that I want to do anyway!

PQ: Could you give us the title of a paperback book for which the cover painting required an amount of research comparable to that done for "Hero"?

KF: Gee, that would be hard. There must be one. The book we were just talking about, for instance, EMILY GOODE. It did not require that kind of research; but I did go to Philadelphia to look at the gates because the 1876 Centennial Exhibition was an important part of the mechanism of the story. I also researched the machine pictured that powered the other machinery. That is an adapted version to fit my own particular problems. The clockworks, of course, are reasonably accurate. The coin is the actual 1861 coin; it was, in that case, researched very carefully. Similarly, my painting of CASTAWAYS IN TIME was painted very loosely; and it really didn't matter too much. But each of the costumes in it is authentic for its character.

PQ: In your lecture this afternoon, you mentioned that much of the color and detail of a painting is lost in reproduction. What techniques are used in printing to get a reproduction to be as faithful as possible to the painting?

KF: Well, the final arbiter is the pressman. If he doesn't handle his presses exactly right, or with precisely the right flow, the right density, of blue ink as compared to the density of yellow and red that he's putting in, he's going to throw the whole thing off. Or the worst thing that can happen to you with a picture like ZENYA [DAW #115, by E.C. Tubb], you can imagine the density of the black ink. If you overrate the black ink the least bit it washes out every bit of color; and all you've got is a black mud. Everything is dull. But then in addition to that, you've got to have an absolutely perfect register or you lose the vibrancy which is the essential part of the texture of Zenya's skin.

PQ: Do you remember any other covers for paper-back books that were as difficult to reproduce as ZENYA was?

KF: Oh, yes. Lots of them are. It depends again on whether they're doing a high speed job or something else. In doing our own prints; for example, the one for SINS OF THE FATHERS (originally an

ASTOUNDING cover) was printed first in a straight four-color process. But the reds simply did not have the vibrancy they needed, so we added three different shades: an orangish red, and almost purplish red, and one somewhere in between those two. What you're actually getting is the quality of glazing that you get in oil paints because this is layer on layer with the dots offset just the least bit in each case so that each color underneath vibrates the most intense red that you'll ever find. You wouldn't find it in anything except custom work.

PQ: So instead of four-color printing, you did a seven-color process to get the reds correctly vibrant in SINS OF THE FATHERS.

KF: Yes, that's right. READER'S DIGEST, you probably know, may run as high as seventeen colors to get their illustrations.

PQ: Now does that mean that each page with seventeen colors has to be run through the presses seventeen times?

KF: No, it goes through the press once. That's the astonishing thing about this. The pressman can handle the correct flow of seventeen inks. Think of the genius you've got to have running the presses to print millions of copies and have them come out good!

PQ: You mentioned also that you own your company that reproduces your prints that are for sale here.

KF: No, the company is ours, but we have the prints done by an outfit that does a lot of work for NATIONAL GEOGRAPHIC, and for years did work for the National Museum. They were in Richmond; they are now in Baltimore. They're probably the best around.

PQ: We were interested that you said one reason for starting your print company was so that you could get eight colors as opposed to four-color printing.

KF: Also, generally speaking, a good pressman will enjoy working with a special company like ours. Because it gives him a chance to use his artistry, to show what he can do. My printer on these prints twice won prizes from the Printing Institute of the Virginias, which is a very prestigious regional prize. I was a fair-haired boy with him after that!

PQ: In your comments this afternoon, you've said things like "The readers wouldn't like that" or "The reader expects that." When you're doing a painting, do you think in terms of the reader's expectations, or the author's intention, or your own impressions?

KF: All three. The author's intention comes first, and what the reader wants or hopes to get is second. All of my thinking on covers is from the viewpoint of the reader because I am a reader first and then an illustrator second.

PQ: Do you think very many illustrators think in those terms?

KF: Some do. Probably the majority does not. It's the difference between say George Proctor's approach and Roger Stine's approach. Roger goes at each job as a technical problem. It doesn't matter what you give him, he's going to give you a more or less dispassionate treatment of it. Whereas, George is much more inclined to say, "No, I don't like this idea. If we can't do it my way, we won't do it at all. This is the way it should be done! I'm the artist; take it!" He doesn't approach things quite that way, but I'm sure that he thinks in those terms. To a certain extent I do myself. If I don't want to do monsters, I'm not going to do monsters. At one point, I felt that it was bad for children to be exposed to all of this horrible sort of thing (after I had done a good many of them). So I simply quit doing it. Ballantine wanted me to do some when I came back from Mexico in '63. They wanted me to do a series of horror books of that sort. And I simply said, "No, I'm not doing that sort of thing."

PQ: You don't do horror paintings at all any more?

KF: No, when I have an opportunity to handle aliens, I don't want to treat them negatively. Even when I have to handle a monster, I like to treat it as a more or less sympathetic creature. I think it's very important that we convey to the public an image to counteract the movie image of the aliens. Because we are going to meet them. And if you have--as I've said in some speech or other--suppose the visiting alien turns out to be a six-foot intelligent spider; you are going to be a little bit prejudiced in your dealings with him. And I think the more we can get away from creating prejudice and fear, the better off we're going to be.

PQ: So you see a need for a sense of social responsibility in an artist?

KF: Oh, yes. I mean, if an artist is not a part of his culture, he's not an artist anyway. And he makes his contribution to that particular culture by his work--what he does for commercial use, you might say. If he wants to paint for himself only, that's another matter.

PQ: Art for art's sake?

JOHN BRUNNER
THE
STARDROPPERS

NEW WORLDS
OF FANTASY
edited by Terry Carr

imagination goes wild
in today's best tales
of the strange, by

ROGER ZELAZNY
JOHN
BRUNNER
J. G.
BALLARD
THOMAS M.
DISCH
AVRAM DAVIDSON

He summoned the monsters of the
past to help him rule the world
TIMESCOOP
by John Brunner

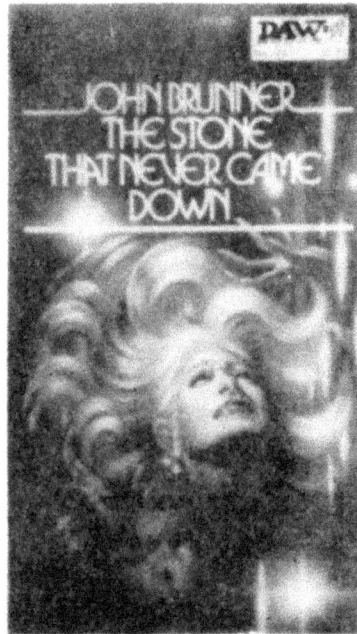

DAW
JOHN BRUNNER
THE STONE
THAT NEVER CAME
DOWN

KF: That's an artist's business, but it has nothing to do with his social responsibility.

PQ: So what you were saying earlier is that you hope your cover art will help promote toleration for beings different from ourselves, such as intelligent spiders?

KF: I don't know that "toleration" is quite the word. We may find ourselves in a position that we are the ones being tolerated.

PQ: But wouldn't your art promote the idea of being more tolerant of all sorts of differences?

KF: Perhaps, certainly art can help prevent us from being shocked quite as easily.

PQ: Talking about sympathetic aliens, I noticed that the robot in "Who" is particularly sympathetic, his eyes especially. Is that one of your favorites?

KF: No. It's one of my best known, but not necessarily one of my favorites.

PQ: You say it's one of your best known; has it been used by several different publishers?

KF: No, but it was used for the ASTOUNDING anthology, the CANDLE FOR MARIO volume. And then it was used in a modernized version, with the band dripping out of the robot's hand, by the rock group "Queen" for one of their album covers.

PQ: We've talked about artistic freedom in pulp versus paperback work; but comparatively, do you find paperback, hardback, or magazine publishers to offer the greatest financial incentives to the artist? Or is there a distinction?

KF: There is a most decided distinction. The

book jacket is a pleasure to do; and it has a certain amount of prestige, I suppose. But for the prices they pay, I can't afford to do them. I'll stick with paperbacks.

PQ: You mentioned that you deplore the nostalgia that demands cover art imitative of that in the pulps of the 20's and 30's. But you say that the "Golden Age" of science fiction was 1939-45. When you say "Golden Age" do you mean in fiction content or in art?

KF: I'm talking about fiction content. I won't even put down the artwork, because there was some superb artwork being done in ASTOUNDING.

PQ: So you wouldn't mind nostalgia for the art of 1939-45, but you object to a nostalgia going on back to the 20's and 30's?

KF: My objection isn't even to the nostalgia. My objection is that I think that art deco was just about the absolute nadir of design.

PQ: Do you know off-hand how many paperback publishers you've done cover for? You've mentioned Ballantine, Avon, and DAW.

KF: A couple of Signets...

PQ: How many Ace covers have you done?

KF: Oh, at last count, I think it was around 96 for Ace....Then there were several for Avon that I did much later in the game. I did some for that man in California, Maurice Jarodius, for what eventually became the Freeway Press. I did several for them. And let's see, there were several other publishers I did covers for. Back in the late 50's several companies came and went over-night. You'd do two or three things for them and

33

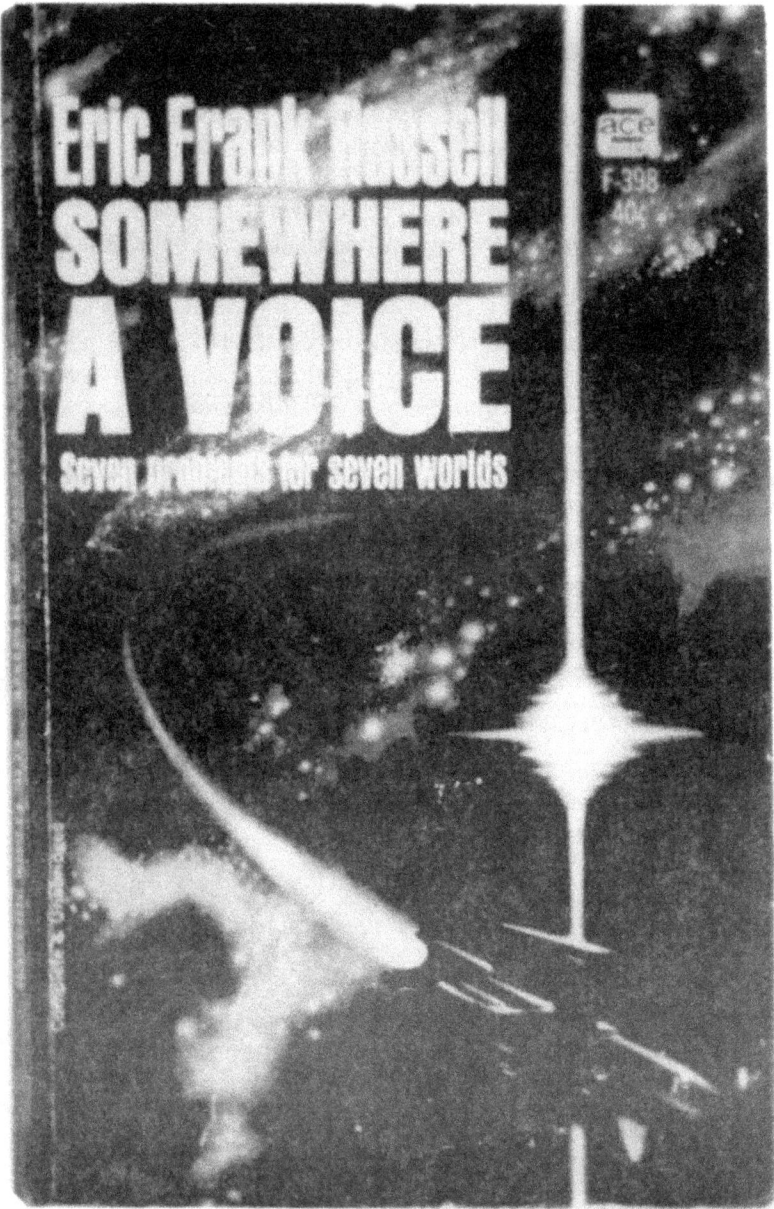

Eric Frank Russell
SOMEWHERE
A VOICE
Seven problems for seven worlds

ace
F-398
40¢

never hear from them again. Lion Books, for instance; I did one or two for them. As a matter of fact it was the art director of Lion Books that had me "filed" as a fantasy artist and wouldn't let me do any other kind of work.

PQ: Do you remember his name?

KF: No, and it's probably just as well!

PQ: What are some of your favorite paperback covers and why?

KF: That's awfully hard to say. I've always been very fond of the cover for SOMEWHERE A VOICE. And as a matter of fact, I think the starfield in that is one of the prettiest starfields I ever painted. I tried to get that quality in others and never quite achieved it.

My all time favorite ASTOUNDING cover is "Pirates of Ersatz," probably because of the subject matter. Esthetically or technically it's reasonably satisfying even though the reproduction is loose. But just the whole concept of this one amused me very much. I'm sorry I ever let the original out of my hands.

PQ: Did you ever get the kind of recognition as an artist that you got with your by-line promi- nently displayed on the covers of Lancer Books from any other paperback publisher?

KF: No, it's hard enough to even keep them from painting or cropping out your signature.

PQ: As paperback collectors, we want to know who the cover artist is. So often the artist's name is not only left off the cover painting but also is nowhere to be found in the book. And the publishers won't cooperate. Either they have kept no records of the artists or else they don't want to go to the trouble of looking through their records.

KF: I know. I've struggled for years with publishers over this issue of artist recognition. I got Ace to do it finally. And I believe DAW has started giving the artist's name. But it's like pulling teeth!

PQ: When you paint covers for any of these books, do you have a set size that you work with?

KF: Oh, yes. I established a size, which is actually 15" x 20" simply because that would fit into a case that I could slip under an airplane seat. And I wasn't about to send my paintings through as baggage! I was traveling back and forth every week or ten days; and actually carrying a portfolio that big got some odd looks, but nothing bigger than that would do. Actually, in a way, I'm a frustrated miniaturist. I would be really happy if I could do everything small.

PQ: Have you ever done anything in miniature and had it blown up for the cover of a paperback book?

KF: As a matter of fact, yes. I think this one, FROM THIS DAY FORWARD, by John Brunner, was a blow-up. Working with a painting no bigger than that gives a very nice, loose, painterly effect which I probably couldn't have achieved by trying to do it oversize.

Recent Releases

Allen Lane: King Penguin, A Biography by J.E.
Morpurgo. Hutchinson of London, 1979.

The history of the growth and development of
20th-century paperback publishing has run a par-
allel course in both England and the United States.
Each country was influenced by cheap 19th-century
publishing practices in their respective countries
as well as by Tauchnitz and Albatross Books, which
were distributed in Germany. Each was aware of
successful practices--editorial, design and mark-
eting--of the other.

The first successful English paperback publisher in this century was Penguin Books, which
issued its first list in 1935. Four years later
Pocket Books published its first list of ten titles.
Both imprints were preceded by numerous unsuccessful
attempts to reach mass audienced with quality lit-
erature at lower prices.

J.E. Morpurgo's ALLEN LANE: KING PENGUIN is
both a biography of the founder and first head of
Penguin Books and also of the company. Hardbound,
in the familiar shade of orange buckram for which
Penguin is still associated, the volume first
centers on uncle, John Lane and his Bodley Head
publishing house. Both were models for Allen Lane,
and their influence appears never to have completely disappeared from his life.

The author details the early years of Penguin
when Allen Lane and his two brothers time and again
defied the cautious and opposition of other English
publishers and booksellers by successfully disign-
ing and marketing series after series of imagina-
tive original and reprinted publications for a
world-wide reading audience. Lane's relationships
with figures in American softcover publishing,

among them Ian Ballantine, Kurt Enoch and Victor
Weybright, all of whom worked at one time for Lane
and later founded softcover companies of their own,
are discussed, though not as thoroughly as an
American reader would wish. Lane, a brilliant
predictor of reading tastes and marketer of books,
with a deep sensitivity to good book design, was
at the same time moody and unpredictable in his
business and personal relationships. Personnel
decisions made by Lane at Penguin seem to have con-
tinually been touched by both whimsey and naivete.
        Morpurgo, a former Penguin employee and head
of the trade association of English book publishers,
is also father-in-law to Lane's eldest daughter.
Although not on speaking terms with Lane at the
time of the publisher's death, the author seems to
have made an honest attempt to weigh the contributions of both publisher and publishing house to the
culture of English-speaking nations. Despite the
fact that he has never heard of the simple declar-
ative sentance, Morpurgo is successful in establishing the importance of the publishing house and
its founder.
        The book is a must for any serious student
of 20th-century book publishing and paperbacks.
It is unfortunate, however, that its high price tag
(I paid over $25 for an imported edition) mocks the
very man who reached "the million" by selling his
Penguins for 6 pence each.
                    ------Thomas L. Bonn

ZANE GREY'S WEST Beginning Publication

Repairing Paperbacks
by Nicholas Willmott

Opinions vary as to the advisability of repairing collectable paperbacks. A friend of mine,
a keen fellow collector, rigorously believes that
a book should be preserved in the state acquired,
warts and all. In the case of a particularly
scarce item this may be advisable as incautious
meddling can court disaster. Nevertheless my own
view is that, with care, much can be done to redeem
otherwise deplorable copies, at least until a
better replacement can be found. To this end,
over the past couple of years, I have experimented
with various techniques and have met with moderate
success. Before going into detail I must mention
that extreme care must be exercised at all times as,
from bitter experience, it is only too easy to ruin
a copy beyond all hope -- I would not like to be
held responsible for the demise of somebody's
prized JUNKIE!

For repair work a good supply of glue is essential. Ideally this should be a proper binder's
glue with a neutral pH value. For practical pur-
poses a good quality commercial gum is quite ade-
quate provided any visible surplus is quickly removed; Otherwise faint stains result. Scotch tape
is anathema and should never be used for any repair
jobs. A sharp craft knife is also handy and a useful asset is a quantity of scrap paperbacks suit-
able only for cannibalisation and experiment.

Starting from the outside, paperback covers
are seldom found in mint condition. As the inner
surface of the cover is not visible tears can
readily be repaired by backing with plain paper or,
if you can get hold of some, Japanese lens tissue.
Holes can be treated in the same way and, if des-

["Repairing Paperbacks" originally appeared in PENGUIN COLLECTORS' SOCIETY NEWSLETTER,
November 13, 1979 under the title "Repairing Penguins."]

ired, a cosmetic effect can be achieved by inking in the missing portions with appropriately matched colors. Weak or detached hinges can similarly be reinforced with a folded strip of paper. The making good of paperback covers is always worthwhile as they can then continue to fulfil their function of protecting the book within.

Paperback covers are often in a grubby condition but they can usually be cleaned, at least partially. Surface stains must be distinguished from yellowing caused by chemical changes in the paper. Unfortunately little can be done about that. A soft eraser can then be used but care should be taken not to disturb the surface texture of the paper. It is surprising how much grime can thus be removed but it is a job that must be done thorouthly if streaks are to be avoided. Finger marks tend to be more resistant but they can often be removed with dry cleaning solvent. When using this sort of substance the area being cleaned must be backed with several layers of blotting paper, otherwise the stain is liable to spread through the book. Dry cleaning solvent is very effective in removing wax crayon marks.

I have had little success to date in removing ink or felt-tip marks. They only respond to solvents so powerful that print is also bleached and the paper damaged.

Paperbacks with glossy covers can be cleaned by lightly rubbing with a very slightly damp sponge. An excess of water leads to warping of the cover.

The top, botton and fore edges of the book can also be cleaned with an eraser. The book must be squeezed very tightly while this is done or pages are likely to be damaged.

Pages can be cleaned in much the same way as covers always remembering that they are more fragile and prone to damage. All dog-ears should be folded back as a matter of course. It is important that the book is cleaned as much as possible before any gluing takes place.

In many cases it will be found that the original glue used in the assembly of the book has deteriorated with age. This means that cover and spine will often be partially or wholly detached from the body of the book. Unless the defect is slight, in which case fresh glue can be inserted using a sliver of paper, it is best to remove the cover in its entirety. The spine can then be re-glued, after removing any loose fragments of the original glue, and the cover replaced. Any excess glue must be removed and the book placed vertically, spine downwards, while the glue dries.

Weak or torn hinges can also be reinforced by removing the cover as above and lining the inside of the spine area. Problems sometimes arise when relining or patching would obscure advertising or other matter. In this event it is possible to use Japanese lens tissue, which remains transparent after gluing. Under no circumstances be tempted to use scotch tape.

If the front or back cover has become detached it is often easiest to repair by applying glue to its extreme edge. In this way it is possible to replace the cover such that its hinging action is only slightly impaired.

Another problem is encountered when a book has previously been repaired hamfistedly with scotch tape. When this has been done some time ago, the scotch tape will often have dried out and can be carefully peeled off, but it generally leaves a yellow stain. Sometimes scotch tape can be removed with dry cleaning solvent but use special care not to damage the cover. Price stickers also respond to this.

A simple job is the replacement of detached pages and plates in recent paperbacks and loose signatures in earlier ones. In all cases the offending leaves can be tipped in. This involves applying the thinnest touch of glue to the extreme edge, opening the book as far as possible, then slotting in the detached page, plate or signature ensuring that all edges are flush with the rest of the book. Again care must be taken to remove any excess glue before standing the book on its spine to dry.

Similarly missing or defective flyleaves can be replaced from cannibalised scrap paperbacks. Obviously the best effect is achieved with the closest matching of the paper's age and quality.

Paperbacks are pliable things and if stored incorrectly can become warped. Paperbacks acquired in such a distorted state require pressing. Ideally a professional nipping press should be used but I have had success using an improvised press consisting of a pair of smooth boards held between fretworkers' G-clamps. The book should be gently eased into the right shape and then left in the press under moderate pressure for a few days. Pressing is also useful after any major repair job.

These notes give some indication of the sort of techniques I have been using. I am still not satisfied that I am achieving the best possible results but some progress is being made. It is difficult to lay down hard and fast rules as no two repair jobs are identical and each case must be weighed on its merits. It is frequently best to leave well enough alone. While it is next to impossible to convert a mediocre copy of a paperback to a fine one, it is not difficult to improve a book that would otherwise be fit only for the trash. This flexible attitude to repair would seem to be the only answer to the increasing scarcity of early paperbacks in good condition.

Quotable Quotes

After the basic necessities of life there is nothing more precious than books. FOURNIER, 1764

Interior Paperback Art
by Mark Schaffer

Paperback history is cyclical, as the curious 70's revival of early fifties swashbuckling romances has made clear. One wonders if the industry will quickly exhaust its current affair with pee-kaboo flaps, peephole covers, and cinemascopic foldout gimmicks, and revive the illustrated paperback, a staple of the late forties and early fifties, and ripe for a new life in this "visual" age.

On the face of it, the idea of sticking accompanying illustrations into pocket books seems logical enough, and certainly provided a nice selling point. Not only A TALE OF TWO CITIES for a quarter, but cute little sepia drawings just like its $5.00 big brother. In those long-dead days, the paperback tried to be both an inexpensive duplication of the original writ small and a catchy extension of the hardback. Since this required the same attention to detail and overall graphic concept, it is not unusual to find the obligatory Gluyas Williams' sketches adorning Robert Benchley's Pocket Book reprints, or the famous John Tenniel etchings for Pocket Books' late forties ALICE IN WONDERLAND.

Just as paperback cover art spanned a wide range, so too did the strategies and styles of narrative illustration between the covers. A look at some examples from several eras and publishers will reveal another neglected storehouse for paperback appreciation.

In retrospect, it seems that the illustrated paperback was on the drawing board from the start. Of course, wartime restricktions changed all design and production plans at Pocket Books. Still, a good idea of what De Graff had in mind can be seen in the 1939 BRIDGE OF SAN LUIS REY (Pocket Books #9). A handsomely designed package featuring

43

striking Rockwell Kentish graphics by Amy
Drevenstedt, Wilder's first paperback appearance
prophesised a bright future for paperback graphics
(it is interesting to note that this edition was
published in cooperation with Boni Books, the
thirties precursor of De Graff, and a pioneer in
paperback graphic design. See PQ vol 2, #4 page
26.) But, with the war, all changed, and the 1944
edition reflects the compromises; The quality
graphics were shelved. The earliest edition of
TREASURE ISLAND (Pocket Books #25) had many de-
lightful full page ink illustrations by Gregor
Duncan keyed to the tale, and these didn't survive
1942. Nicolas Bentley's New Yorker-style drawings
for THE BEST OF DAMON RUNYON (Pocket Books #53)
are quintessential renderings of Runyon's special
world. The war had no time for New Yorker whimsy.
Still, it did provide impetus for some highly
original and intriguing paperback art.

Famed correspondant Ernie Pyle's THIS IS YOU
WAR (Pocket Books #274) included many in-text
illustrations of Pyle's grunt-level view of war,
and, even more pointedly, John Hersey's INTO THE

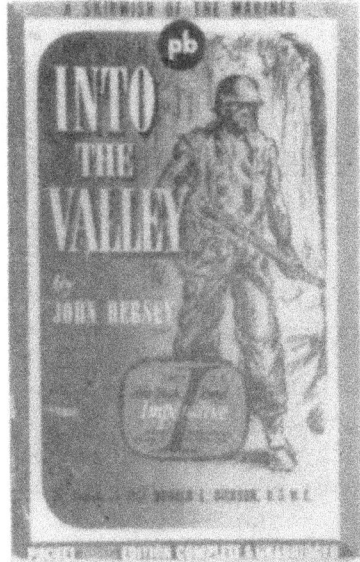

Donald L. Dickson

Donald L. Dickson

interior art of *Into The Valley*   44

GIOVANNI BOCCACCIO

Decameron

Mac Harshberger

Mac Harshberger

interior art of *Decameron*

VALLEY (Pocket Books #225) featured arresting
pencil sketches by Marine Major Donald L. Dixon
that have a lived-in immediacy to them about day-
to-day ware life that surpasses more well known
Life Magazine photojournalism by Smith and others.
　　Postwar Pocket Books attempted to recapture
their earlier polished style, and some of the work
produced during this period did this admirably.
Three of special interest were the Fitzgerald
translation of THE RUBAIYAT OF OMAR KHAYAM (Pocket
Books #128), Boccaccio's THE DECAMERON (Pocket
Books #477), and the 1951 printing of ALICE IN
WONDERLAND (Pocket Books #835). When it came to
prestige products, Pocket Books was the M-G-M of
the industry, as Mac Harshberger's exquisite
sepia-toned illustrations for Boccaccio's ribaldry
attest. For the 1948 printing of THE RUBAIYAT OF
OMAR KHAYAM, Pocket Books commissioned illustrator
Gordon Ross to provide exclusive artwork for the
book, and the result may well be the pinnacle of
paperback illustration. Ross' seventy-five finely
honed plates are a triumph of design, tone, and

45

stylistic mastery that makes this edition totally unique and renders the Avon school of adolescent fantasy paperback illustration in a new light. A treasure. Pocket Books also demonstrated how much fine art could be had for a quarter when they issued ALICE IN WONDERLAND complete with Sir John Tenniel's original ninety-two Victorian etchings from the famous woodcuts.

Other less vaunted styles were encouraged as well: Casey Jones and Bill Crawford's bawdy cartoon work on many of Max Schulman's urban comedies like THE ZEBRA DERBY (Pocket Books #840) pointed directly to the light, cartoony fifties mood, while Edward Shenton's haunting pattern decorations for Hemingway's GREEN HILLS OF AFRICA (Perma #M3056) are a tasteful and provacative touch.

While Pocket Books was trying to recapture past grace, the Bantam rooster came up with something both new and intriguing and, in its own way, as unique as some Pocket Books efforts. Beginning in early 1946, Bantam began to feature curious inner leaf end-paper illustrations on its editions. Although in some ways reminiscent of Dell's mapback aerial views, as on Francis Allan's FIRST COME, FIRST KILL (Bantam #34), the stylistic range and aesthetic imagination was as broad as the new company's cover illustration experiments. Some highlights of this brief (Bantam discontinued the end-paper art in 1947) but provacative subgenre follow.

Frederick Lewis Allen's ONLY YESTERDAY (Bantam #27) is an ex-

Arnold

cellent example of the boldness of Bantam's
graphic ideas. The inner leaf papers contain a
college-like arrangement of actual newspaper headlines that pinpoint in an eye-catching way the
milestones in Allen's post World War I popular
history. This "tabloid" style, with strong echos
of Dos Passos, was used again in Gene Fowler's
THE GREAT MOUTHPIECE (Bantam #32) -- the inner
leaves emblazoned with headlines trumpeting the
manhunt for Bill Fallon, the notorious crooked
lawyer. Semidocumentary was a big late forties
trend, and Bantam was most adept at visualising
their product with contemporary punch.

Other genres were given fresh slants as well,
James Hiton's neglected crime masterpiece WAS IT
MURDER? (Bantam #29) has an eerie cap and gown
hovering ghost-like over a staid British boy's
school in an almost cinematic perspective. Other
mysteries, like Mary Collins' THE FOG COMES (Bantam
#23) and Ruth Wallis' NO BONES ABOUT IT (Bantam
#72) are illustrated in mapback-style panoramas.
The Wallis is particularly interesting in that the

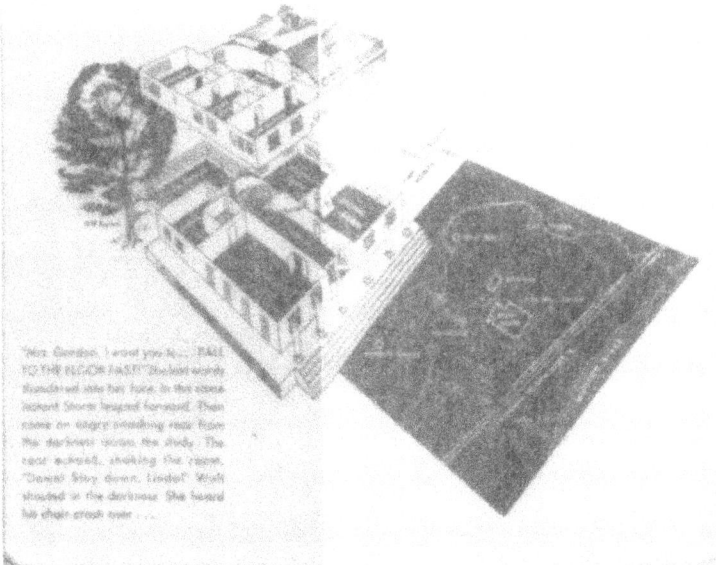

interior cover of *First Come First Kill*

47

inner leaf graphics feature a typical mystery novel residential street, but the artist's point of view is a Wellesian establishing shot as from a crane. Over and over, it seems that Bantam artists were stylistically more in tune than the competition with aesthetic influences from other mediums. John Hersey's A BELL FOR ADANO (Bantam #45) suggests a like movie approach in its inner leaf high angle panorama of Adano Square. It appeared that Bantam was attempting to "open up" the paperback's vista with these double-leaf illustrations. Bantam's historical pageant novel reprints were other good examples of this impulse: Howard Fast's CITIZEN TOM PAINE (Bantam #30) featured a map of mid-1700 America, and Grace Zarring Stone's THE COLD JOURNEY (Bantam #44) is introduced by an almost satellite angle view of the book's vast canvas. It is almost as if Bantam wanted to extend Dell's map approach to encompass whole continents, as Francis Yeats

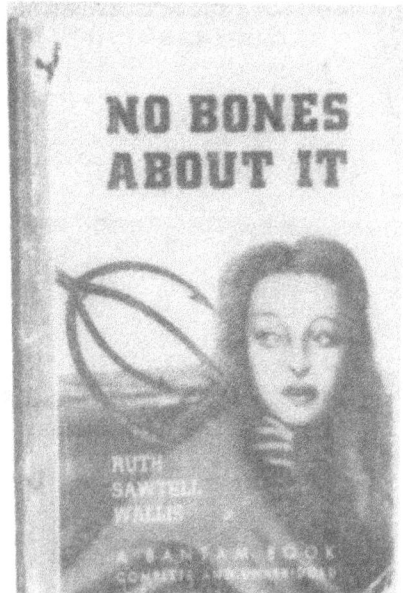

Zoffman

48

interior cover of *Was It murder?*

interior cover of *No Bones About It*

interior cover of *A Bell for Adano*

interior cover of *Citizen Tom Paine*

Cal Diehl

Charles Andres

Brown's LIVES OF A BENGAL LANCER (Bantam #43) ably demonstrates. One can almost hear the old, familiar Warner Bros. voice over hundreds of Saturday afternoon adventure flicks, setting the geographic stage before Errol Flynn strode on screen. It's no wonder that Bantams were the first paperbacks to resemble movie posters in the fifties.

But the rooster could do excellent work in miniature scale as well. Glenway Westcott's APARTMENT IN ATHENS (Bantam # 87) featured a dramatic scene from the novel that sums up the menace of political repression in the story, and Steinbeck's CANNERY ROW (Bantam #75) echos the Kent-like graphic themes of Pocket Books' BRIDGE OF SAN LUIS REY.

The Bantam experiment with end-paper art was intriguing and showed how savvy the new company was. The decision to discontinue it was probably based on cost, although the basic idea would survive, as Bantam's fifties covers became more broad-canvassed and filmic. In some ways, the inner art wound up on the outside covers.

51

Two other striking ex-
amples of the art can be
found in Melville's TYPEE
(Avon #T117) which features
dense, dream-like render-
ings of island life in all
its sensousness, and J.
Hasek's THE GOOD SOLDIER
SCHWEIK (Penguin #572) has
superb interior drawings
in a primitive woodcut
style by Joseph Lada rem-
iniscent of nothing but
themselves, unique art for
a unique book.

This article concen-
trates on the early history
of paperbacks. But today
interior art is still an
important aspect of trade
and speciality paperbacks
particularly heroic fan-
tasy and science fiction.

interior cover of
The Lives of a Bengal Lancer

First International

American Paperback Cover Art Exhibition

Early in 1978, a small group of people met together to lay groundwork which after years of hard work and thousands of miles of travel will bear fruit early next year. From January 17 to March 7 of 1981, the first international **American paperback Cover Art Exhibition** will be held at Gemeentemusem (Municipal Museum) The Hague, Holland. The exhibit will focus on the art and design of American paperbacks and their covers.

Accompanying the exhibit, a 250-300 page catalogue entitled *Paperbacks, USA: A Graphic History, 1939-1959* will be published. The catalogue will have 32 pages of color illustrations and many many black & white reproductions. The first part of the catalogue will consist of a short history of European paperbacks and American paperbacks in the 19th and 20th century. the second part will focus entirely on the cover art: the general development of cover styles, different artists in different periods, recurring themes, movie tie-ins, dust jackets, re-drawn covers, the function of art directors, artistic influences, recognition of cover art, and some remarks from artists themselves. The third part will consist of various appendices, a year-by-year account from 1939-1959, a register of paperback publishers, and an illustrated register of paperback cover artists.

Piet E. Schreuders, a free-lance disigner and publisher of two magazines, will be editor of the catelogue. More details on the exhibit and the availability of the *Paperbacks, USA* catelogue will be announced soon.

Will Buy or Trade

Special Wants: Avon 178 *Fast One* by Paul Cain
Avon 496 *Fast One* by Paul Cain
Avon 268 *Seven Slayers* by Paul Cain
Also need Dell bookracks.

Bill Lyles
77 High St.
Greenfield, MA 01301

Book Sellers

The following people sell paperbacks. Most mail out booklists on a regular basis and all are knowledgeable paperback bibliophiles. For specific wants write directly to the addresses below and please include S.A.S.E.

BILL & PAT LYLES
77 High St.
Greenfield, MA 01301
(413) 774-2432

SCOTT OWEN
P.O. BOX 343
Moraga, CA 94556

GRAVESEND BOOKS
Box 235
Poconopines, PA 18350

JUDY K. REYNOLDS
9969 B Sloanes Sq.
St. Louis, MO 63134
(314) 429-6654

JEFF MEYERSON
50 First Place
Brooklyn, N.Y. 11231

JACK IRWIN
16 Gloucester Lane
Trenton, N.J. 11231

FANTASY ARCHIVES
71 Eight Ave.
New York, N.Y. 10014

BILL LIPPINCOTT
Dunbar Hill Rd.
North Anson, ME 04958

MICHAEL BARSON
117 Crosby St.
Haverhill, MA 01830

JAN LANDAU
Rt 2 Box 293
New Castle, Virginia 24018

FAMILY PAPERBACKS
4016 Central Ave. N.E.
Minneapolis, MN 55412

BILL LOESER
P.O. BOX 1702
New Bern, NC 28560

ED KALB
3227 E. Enid Ave.
Mesa, Arizona 85204
(602) 830-1855

JEFF PATTON
3621 Carolina St., N.W.
Massillon, OH 44646

McCLINTOCK BOOKS
P.O. Box 3111
Warren, OH 44485

BUNKER BOOKS
P.O. BOX 1638
Spring Valley, CA 92077
(714) 469-3296

PAPERBACK PARADISE
468 Centre St.
Jamaica Plain, MA 02130

BARRY & WALLY PATTENGIL
Rt 3 Box 508
Waco, Texas 76708

THE OLD BOOK STORE
210 E. Cuyahoga Falls Ave.
Akron, OH 44310

MURDER BY THE BOOK
194½ Atwells Ave.
Providence, RI 02903

GALE SEBERT
Sebert's Books
Leivasy, WV 26676

LUCILE COLEMAN
P.O. BOX 610813
North Miami, FL 33161

PANDORA'S BOOKS LTD
Box 86
Neche, ND 58265

MOSTLY MYSTERIES BOOKS
398 St. Clair Avenue East
Toronto, Ontario M4T 1P5

If you are a bookseller and would like you name and address printed in "Book Sellers," please drop us a line. Please tell us if you sell paperbacks by mail and/or have a retail store. We are also interested if you mail out lists on a regular basis. Happy Paperback Hunting!

fantasy newsletter

The Monthly News Magazine
of the Fantasy & Science Fiction Field

With the mushrooming of the Science Fiction/Fantasy field over the last few years, it has become increasingly difficult to keep abreast with the Science Fiction/Fantasy scene. One magazine which has succeeded is FANTASY NEWSLETTER.

Displaying one of the most professional layouts of any magazine in this genre, FANTASY NEWSLETTER takes its subscribers each month on a personal tour to meet the books and the bookmen;the trade and the mass-market; the fan press and the New York publisher; the authors and the illustrators. From Science Fiction/Fantasy movies to Specialty Publishers to indept interviews with your favorite authors, FANTASY NEWSLETTER puts it all together, packaged in its own original cover art.

FANTASY NEWSLETTER provides total coverage with sections like....

The Outlook, Specialty Publisher's, Trade Books, Mass-market Paperbacks, Fan Press, On Fantasy with Karl Edward Wagner/ Fritz Leiber, *Editorials, Book Reviews, Interviews, and Science Fiction/Fantasy Convention coverage.*

Remenber, for comprehensive Science Fiction/Fantasy coverage turn to the Monthly News Magazine of the Fantasy & Science Fiction Field, **FANTASY NEWSLETTER.**

For only $12.00 you will recieve 12 generously illustrated issues keeping you informed of the total Science Fiction/Fantasy scene. All copies are mailed in a sturdy envelope. Send all correspondence, queries, and subscriptions to Paul C. Allen, 1015 West 36th St. Loveland, Colorado 80537.

Subscribe Today!

★ ★

PENGUIN COLLECTORS
SOCIETY

Those interested in paperback publishing history should be aware of the **PENGUIN COLLECTORS' SOCIETY**. Based in London, **PCS** was organized in 1974 and provides its members with two yearly newsletters devoted to the man and the publisher who started it all, Allen Lane and Penguin.

The most recent issue, May 1980, features The Penguin Modern Classics; a reprinting of Allen Lane's Books for the Million; an article on the German paperback line, The Albatross; and an informative notes section.

Also published this Spring by **PCS** is THE KING PENGUIN SERIES by David J. Hall. This superb checklist/bibliography of the King Penguin paperbacks lists price, designer, reprints, and printer & type and includes informative annotations throughout. This **PCS** edition (limited to 300 copies) has justified margins and includes four plates.

Annual membership/subscription is $3.50 per year (to USA). Make checks payable to **Penguin Collector's Society** and send to Richard Smith, 30 Alexandra Grove, London N. 4.

Worthy of Your Support

—

PAPERBACK QUARTERLY is now available for wholesale distribution. The purchase of ten copies (minimum) costs $12.00 and retails for $20.00. All copies are returnable at dealers expense for full refund. Payment must accompany orders. Write to PAPERBACK QUARTERLY, 1710 Vincent St., Brownwood, Texas 76801.

www.ingramcontent.com/pod-product-compliance
Lightning Source LLC
Chambersburg PA
CBHW021225020426
42331CB00003B/476